How to Overcome Rejection

The Most Effective Strategies for Dealing with Rejection, Building Confidence, and Designing the Life You Deserve

By John Baskin

John Baskin

John Baskin

<u>Disclaimer Notice:</u>

Please note the information contained within this document is for educational and entertainment purposes only. Every attempt has been made to provide accurate, up to date and reliable complete information. No warranties of any kind are expressed or implied. Readers acknowledge that the author is not engaging in the rendering of legal, financial, medical or professional advice.

By reading this document, the reader agrees that under no circumstances are we responsible for any losses, direct or indirect, which are incurred as a result of the use of information contained within this document, including, but not limited to, —errors, omissions, or inaccuracies.

Discretion: I am just a passionate student of health & wellness and am looking for the most cutting edge strategies that can benefit my life, which inspires me to share this knowledge to anyone willing to listen.

Author's Note: I realize that my words will not resonate with every reader. As a man committed to constant and never-ending improvement, if you have any <u>constructive feedback</u> that you would like to offer, or feel like the content in my book can be <u>improved</u> in any way...

...please feel free to contact me at:

<u>faithinknowledge@bookenthuziast.com</u>

John Baskin

Table of Contents

Introduction

I commend you for using your personal power to invest in *How to Overcome Rejection: the Most Effective Strategies for Dealing With Rejection, Building Confidence, and Designing the Life You Deserve.* It may have just taken one click to purchase, but it was a commitment, however slight and has the grand potential of transforming the way you perceive the whole concept of 'rejection.'

The substance that lies in these pages will lay out specific and effective strategies to understand how you deal with rejection right now and how to rewire your mind to view rejection as a part of the road to success.

You see, the feeling of rejection stems from a representation of a situation, and the beautiful thing is that we are entirely in control of how we represent anything, and that is the grand gift of being human. We have the ability to create meaning at any instant.

Brimming with wisdom, this book will resonate with your compelling desire to:

- • Grasp opportunities that you know in your gut will put you on a road of fulfillment

- • Understand who you are and consciously decide where you are headed, so that petty distractions and self-conscious impulses are brought into awareness but not entertained

- • Align with your potential because you, first and foremost, believe in your potential and seek proven strategies to instill it in every cell of your body and access it with each decision you make

- • Live life on your terms because anything less will be a disservice to your integrity

This book will take you on an adventure and will educate you to take on new challenges in gradual progression. Before anything can be achieved and withstand the test of time, it requires a resilient mind and owning up to the idea of rejection by recognizing who you are to become. Who you are to become will be the foundation for tackling the so-called challenges of dealing with rejection. In addition, new associations revolving around this sensitive subject will develop so that we take these concepts in the following pages and embody them versus mere intellectualization.

I am excited for this journey you are embarking on and I sincerely thank you for downloading this gem. My intention is that the following specific strategies will be spectacularly beneficial in the long haul, as life is short and you want to experience all that life is filled with before your final days.

Now, let's equip you with massive resilience.

John Baskin

Part One
Understanding Rejection

John Baskin

Chapter One

Overcoming Rejection

In this chapter, you will learn how to:

- Accept rejection

- Transform rejection into opportunity

- Solve rejection in two ways

The Reality of Rejection

"The first story is about connecting the dots... Again, you can't connect the dots looking forward; you can only connect them looking backwards. So you have to trust that the dots will somehow connect in your future. You have to trust in something — your gut, destiny, life, karma, whatever."

-Steve Jobs, 2005

Rejection can happen everywhere and to everyone. People get rejected in their personal lives, such as in school, love, relationships, friendships and even family. Their professional lives too are affected by rejection, an unaccepted proposal, a declined job application or a failed partnership or negotiation. Nobody is also excused from rejection, whether you are rich or poor, young or old, male or female, famous and important or unknown and insignificant, people get rejected all the time.

It hurts too. The feelings associated with rejection involve sadness, loneliness and even anger and depression. Behaviors such as crying, aggression and weakness are also present. This is because as humans, we have this natural need for acceptance. Since each of us have our own limitations, we seek others to bridge the gap of our limitations. When we are rejected, it is as if our nature, physical, mental and social being is threatened. This threat becomes so real that it becomes painful. This is why we react the way we do when we are rejected. However hard we try to hide our feelings, our entire being screams for acceptance, if not at least relief.

Rejection is usually outside our control but our emotions, feelings and behaviors are entirely within our power. You must now allow it to impede on your happiness, character and destiny. Rejection must not derail you in your journey. Yes, it will always be there but so does your confidence, your fortitude and your passion to carry you through and stand triumphant when rejection occurs.

The succeeding chapters will share with you not how to avoid rejection but how to experience it properly and how to overcome it victoriously.

Transformation into an Opportunity

"I think that you have to believe in your destiny; that you will succeed, you meet a lot of rejection and it is not always a straight path, there will be detours- so enjoy the view."

-Michael York

The first step in overcoming rejection is to transform it. When others see rejection as something negative, like a pitfall or an obstacle, you must change your perspective of it. Instead, try a different outlook on rejection. See it as something positive, it is a detour to something better or a stepping stone to something higher. In short and even if it is an ironic statement, accept rejection. Use it as an opportunity to explore alternatives, however slight.

When you are able to shift into this way of thinking, the other steps for overcoming rejection become possible. This shift is the most important step to achieve this feat. I call it a feat because it will not be an easy journey for you. Rejection may not be as painful as before, but it will still hurt. When you encounter the aches, you may feel discouraged or choose to quit in your journey towards overcoming rejection. Before you do, think of what you will miss, you may never be able to be the person you are meant to be, you may not be able to fulfill your purpose or destiny or you may not be able to live the life you have always wanted or deserve to have. Push forward and march on, do it not only for yourself but also for your family and loved ones who count on you to overcome rejection.

The Two Solutions: Short term Relief & Long Term Resilience

"When there is no struggle, there is no strength."
-Oprah Winfrey

The road to overcoming rejection begins with transforming it. The next steps involve two major principles to completely overcome it. These are:

1. Short-term relief

2. Long-term resilience

Short-term relief is the way that can help you cope after the event of a rejection. Regardless of how strong you are, no one is immune to the immediate effects of rejection. These techniques will help you address those feelings and prevent them from entrenching themselves into your thoughts and character. With these coping techniques, you can arrest these feelings and provide you with relief.

Long-term resilience is another way to overcome rejection. This is meant to gradually build on your defenses, to lessen the brunt of the aftermath of rejection. These resilient building techniques will not only protect you in the long run when rejection does occur but it can also prepare you beforehand when rejection is just around the corner.

John Baskin

Chapter Two
Coping Immediately

In this chapter, you will learn how to:

- Use self-talk and positive thinking

- Seek and receive support

- Use physical action to relieve mental aches

Using Self-talk & Positive Thinking

"Keep your face to the sunshine and you cannot see a shadow"
-Helen Keller

Self-talk is a mental exercise used to reframe your thinking. By asking yourself questions, you allow yourself to arrive at answers that will provide insight or even instructions on how to address a situation. Self-talk can be a useful tool when applied to overcoming rejection.

Here are some questions that you can ask yourself when you are fresh from a rejection:

1. What are the reasons behind the rejection?

2. What are the lessons that I can learn from this rejection?

3. What are the alternatives after this rejection?

4. Was I personally rejected or was it my action, output or idea?

5. How long should I feel this pain?

Possible answers from your questions could provide you with a wealth of information that will otherwise remain unknown if you automatically wallowed and focused only on the pain. For example, you may find out that the rejection is justified. There are compelling reasons why you were not chosen. You can use this information to further improve or develop yourself when similar situations occur. If you were rejected on your first option, how about the second, third and other options waiting for you? They could prove to be better alternatives, which otherwise you will not be accepted into if you were not rejected in the first place.

Most people, upon being rejected, feel that it is an attack to themselves and to their character. When you are able to disassociate yourself from your output, you can accept and move on after the rejection. For example, your project proposal was denied. Do not think or say, "I was denied." Instead state it exactly as it is, "The proposal was denied." This way you can differentiate yourself from the consequence. Instead of using your energies and time to blame yourself, you can go back to the proposal and find ways to either revise it or seek others who would accept it.

Immediately after the rejection, whether you have within you the coping skills or the resilience to confront it, chances are you will still feel pain or at least feel upset. Instead of choosing to deny this feeling, it is also important to give yourself time to experience it. Allowing these feelings are healthy because it will allow you time to process and understand it. Choosing to deny yourself of these feelings may only prevent you from learning from the emotions and anticipating your reactions when rejection happens again. However, make sure that you give yourself a limit to feeling these emotions. If you find yourself unable to perform daily tasks because of these feelings, then you have to pick yourself up and move forward.

If you are able to genuinely answer these questions, then you are guaranteed to address rejection in the proper and most advantageous way. Self-talk is a concept borrowed from another technique towards overcoming rejection, which is called positive thinking.

Positivity is a conscious choice when you choose to focus on the bright side of whatever current circumstances you may have and at the same time, when you expect the same goodness on your future situation. You can apply the same principles in overcoming rejection.

For example, you can choose to eliminate the negative associations you have with rejections and instead replace them with positive thoughts and ideas. You can continue to convert statements about rejections. You can formulate your thoughts into something objective and educational instead of personal and emotional.

Action: Make a list of questions similar to the ones given in this section. Now recall the most recent or most painful rejection. Use the situation to answer the questions above. You can also list down the answers too when you have them. Use both lists to reevaluate the rejection and begin your positive approach towards rejection.

Seeking & Receiving Social Support

"Dearer are those who reject us as unworthy, for they add another life; they build a heaven before us whereof we had not dreamed, and thereby supply to us new powers out of the recesses of the spirit, and urge us to new and unattempted performances."

-Ralph Waldo Emerson

Catharsis is a term used to describe the expression of your feelings to someone or something and in so doing, reduce the impact or even relief from the same feelings. You can have a cathartic release of your feelings after rejection by sharing it with someone you can trust.

Having someone, who will genuinely listen to you, will provide you not only an avenue to release your frustration and other feelings but also can give you an objective point of view about the rejection. These are the true friends, who can both encourage you and point out the reasons behind the rejection.

Social support has other benefits in relieving you from the feelings of rejection. They can help you go through the process and prevent you from wallowing into those emotions. On the other hand, make sure that you are careful when you choose people to whom you will share your experience.

John Baskin

Another caution when you seek social support is to avoid airing out your feelings in social media. This is a gray area when you expect encouragement because it is open to the public and you may receive comments or feedback that will only harm or make matters worse for you. If you post something on the Internet, chances are it will stay there forever and may only serve to remind yo of the rejection instead of letting you move on from it.

In the end, as long as you are able to receive support from trusted people, it will serve the purpose of a support system. Whether it is done personally or virtually, this shows that having someone or something to express your feelings can definitely relieve you from the negative feelings after rejection.

Action: Choose among your trusted friends who you will approach when you encounter rejection. Make a list of at least two to three of your friends who have this quality. From this list, make a mutual commitment to support each other and to have each other's back when the time of rejection does come. You can create this pact through any communicative avenue that you are comfortable with, but the primary intention is to solidify this support, to have confidence that you will have one another's back when you go knocking somewhere and rejection answers. This will become the true embodiment of a support system.

Using Breathing, Bathing & Other Physical Relievers

"I am crying over the loss of something I never had. How
ridiculous. Mourning something that never was."
- E.L. James

Sometimes psychological relief, in the form of self-talk and
positive thinking or social relief, in the form of support from
trusted people may not be enough to soothe you from the feelings
of rejection. Sometimes, you have to seek physical relief.

You can try breathing exercises to decrease your heart rate and
lower your blood pressure. This creates a relaxing and calming
effect to an otherwise stressful aftermath. While sitting straight
and keeping your eyes closed, take deep breaths. Inhale through
your nose and exhale through your mouth. As you inhale through
your nose, imagine taking in white light and rest on the phrase,
"positivity in." As you exhale out your mouth, imagine breathing
out all of the toxic thoughts and stresses in life, resting on the
phrase, "toxicity out." Perform this exercise slowly and do this for
up to 5 minutes.

Something warm often balances out the coldness you may feel
after a rejection. You may drink a warm cup of tea or give yourself
a warm bath. This warmth is soothing and has the same effect to

settle the rampant thoughts chaotically running through your mind.

Although it is a temporary solution, distracting yourself with other things can help you cope with the rejection. If you go out to do something different that is not related to the source of rejection, you can help take your mind off of it. You can get out of the office, take a road trip or play your favorite sport. You can start the book you have been meaning to read or buy something you have always wanted. These fun and new experiences can help you not only divert your focus away from the rejection but also make you realize that there are other things in your life other than the rejection.

Action: When you feel stress or anxiety that cause your heart to beat faster, use the breathing technique mentioned above. Experience how effective it is to you. If it is, practice it often until it becomes an automatic response to similar feelings. If it isn't a technique you find effective, research other breathing exercises online and give them a try. There is no one right way to do something. May this breathing exercise mentioned become a window, opening you up to new perspectives and opportunities to grow beyond disempowering impulses the minute rejection strikes.

Chapter Three
Practicing Introspection

In this chapter, you will learn how to:

- Develop your vision, passion and purpose

- Know yourself, your strengths and limitations

- Anticipate rejection and its sources

Developing Your Vision, Passion & Purpose

"Rejection is merely a redirection; a course correction to your
destiny."
- Bryant McGill

Developing resilience is a very important step in overcoming rejection. It will act as a buffer against feeling the full impact of a rejection. If you are able to determine your goal, vision or purpose then you are in a better position to navigate yourself when you encounter rejections. The first step then is to develop your vision or purpose.

Finding your purpose in life is a lifelong endeavor. However, one of the best clues to discovering it is through your passion. The activities, the business, the career or the calling you always have fun doing or feel most passionate about often turn out to be the purpose in your life. So, take a minute to think about what you are passionate about. Write it down. If you are still a little stressed, go back to the previous breathing exercise and do it slowly for 5 minutes. Then come back and ask yourself, "What am I really passionate about? What do I love doing that makes me a better person? What do I do that makes me feel like time just stops?" Write it all down. This will give you an idea of what your purpose in life can be. One important thing to note: your purpose in life can change. Don't stress over it, it merely provides a direction for your decisions. Have fun with your purpose and make sure it brings you joy when you think about it. Your purpose won't be perfect. You will continually refine it. Relax!

Now that you have an idea of what your purpose can be, it is now time to develop your vision. A vision is more than just a thought, it is something that you can describe, measure, put a definite timeframe and even almost see and feel. Use this vision of yourself to determine where you want to be in the immediate and distant future. You can call this vision your destiny, dream, ideal or goal. Regardless of what you call it, use it to as your lighthouse as you steer yourself in your daily life. As you can see, your purpose and vision set a direction for your life with the vision being much more specific – allowing you to more effectively prioritize what's fulfilling rather than always getting carried away with things that you perceive as urgent distractions. If you can keep your focus on the goal, you can accept rejections as part of the journey.

For example, if your vision for yourself is to have that dream job you have always wanted; use that goal when you encounter rejections. If your job application was declined, keep your eye on the goal. Is your dream job still there? It definitely is but maybe it is not just in that company. Are there alternatives? You can only find out if you resume your search.

Action: Develop your vision using the SMART method. This acronym stands for specific, measurable, attainable, relevant and time-bound. Instead of saying dream job, make it SMART. Specify it by saying an executive position. Measure it by saying earning a six-figure salary. Make sure it is attainable based on your qualifications and credentials. Check if your vision is still relevant today. Finally, set a timeframe for it; say 10 or 20 years from now. And remember that your vision will be continually expanding.

Knowing Yourself Using the Johari Window
"A man is but the product of his thoughts; what he thinks, he becomes."

- Mahatma Gandhi

	Known to Self	Not known to Self
Known to others		
Not known to others		

One of the best ways to build your resilience is to discover yourself. If you know what you are capable of and what you are not, then you are in a better position to gauge and adjust yourself should rejection come. You can call up on your strengths to see you through rejection and you can address your limitations before they weigh you down. The Johari Window is an effective assessment tool to discover how much exactly you know about yourself. Although it is done with your peers to help you make an exhaustive assessment, you can also use it on yourself.

The window is a table with two rows and two columns, making four boxes. The first column is labeled as 'known to self' and the other column is 'not known to self.' The first row is labeled 'known to others' and the last row is 'not known to others.'

For the upper left box, ask yourself how much about yourself you know and at the same time, others know too. Adjust the size of this box to represent your public self. For the upper right box, ask yourself, how much about yourself do other people know but you yourself are unaware. Do this for the rest of the boxes.

1 open/free area	blind area	2
hidden area	unknown area	
3		4

Once you are done adjusting the lines of the boxes in the window, you can make a rough approximation of how much you really know about yourself. The wider the first column is the more you know about yourself. When the first column is narrow, it may mean that you still have a lot of things to understand about yourself.

Arena		Blind Spot
independent **intelligent**		adaptable brave clever complex dependable kind knowledgeable loving **observant** searching self-assertive self-conscious sensible witty
Façade		**Unknown**
idealistic introverted reflective		able accepting bold calm caring cheerful confident dignified energetic extroverted friendly giving happy helpful ingenious logical mature modest nervous organised patient powerful proud quiet relaxed religious responsive sentimental shy silly spontaneous sympathetic tense trustworthy warm wise

Regardless of the tool you use, it is important to know yourself and the resources that are at your disposal.

Action: If the first column is narrow, ask the support of your friends in your journey for self-discovery. Ask them to assess you as honestly as they can. Listen and respect their opinions. Use their insights as a new resource when you face rejection.

Here is a list of helpful adjectives that you and your friends can use to assess yourself:

• able	• dependable	• loving	• self-conscious
• accepting	• dignified	• mature	• sensible
• adaptable	• energetic	• modest	• sentimental
• bold	• extroverted	• nervous	• shy
• brave	• friendly	• observant	• silly
• calm	• giving	• organized	• spontaneous
• caring	• happy	• patient	• sympathetic
• cheerful	• helpful	• powerful	• tense
• clever	• idealistic	• proud	• trustworthy
• complex	• independent	• quiet	• warm
• confident	• ingenious	• reflective	• wise
• idealistic	• intelligent	• relaxed	• witty
• independent	• introverted	• religious	
• ingenious	• kind	• responsive	
• intelligent	• knowledgeable	• searching	
• introverted	• logical	• self-assertive	

As an added bonus, this <u>website</u>:

(http://www.selfcreation.com/self-awareness/personal-questions.htm) offers an amazing batch of questions for all areas of your life to drastically expand your self-awareness (I personally have no connection to this particular website, but it added tremendous value to my life when I experienced much anxiety and was very insecure post-graduation).

Anticipating the Sources of Rejection

"A rejection is nothing more than a necessary step in the pursuit of success."

- Bo Bennett

Knowing the place and the time of the battlefield often increases the chances for victory. The same is true for overcoming rejection, as always you have to hope for the best while you are prepared for the worst.

Have a contingency plan in the event of rejection. How will you behave? Where will you go? Who do you talk to? How will you react? When you have this plan, you are better equipped when it happens. It will prevent you from doing something that you will regret in the future or from doing something that will just embarrass you in the moment of the rejection.

You can also augment your preparation by recalling the circumstances when you were rejected. Were you unprepared or pressed for time? Was there a strain in the relationship that ended in rejection? Did your instinct tell you to expect rejection? Once you are able to recollect these circumstances, you can establish a trend. When these factors appear again, rejection may be waiting for you. When you can anticipate it, you are better prepared. The more prepared you are, the faster you can cope and overcome rejection.

Action: Try to remember at least 3 events in your life when you were rejected. Find a pattern or similarities between these 3 events. Use the list as red flags for you to watch out for. For example, you will always get rejected when you approach someone in a shy or awkward state. On your next try, choose to be assertive and confident, check if there are changes. If you are accepted then you found a way to use previous rejections to your advantage. You can watch and read about this simple exercise (http://www.lifenthuziast.com/2014/03/25/emotion-is-created-by-motion/) to understand your physiology during empowering and disempowering states.

Chapter Four
Building Confidence

In this chapter, you will learn how to:

- Know your strengths

- Confront your challenges

- Develop confidence

Celebrating Your Strengths

"I don't have an extraordinary degree of self-confidence, but I know the gift I have been given from God, and I try to share it with as many people as possible."

-Andrea Bocelli

Gaining confidence before and regaining it after rejection occurs is another step towards creating resilience. Everyone has a special talent, skill or gift. Whether it is about the sciences, sports, arts, skills, writing, creating, planning or any other field, you have something that you are good at and that you should be proud of. While you may have weaknesses, it is important to shift your focus away from them.

Strengths and more importantly properly identifying and acknowledging that you have them create defensive barriers against the negative feelings of rejection. Believing in yourself and the internal resources you have will help you overcome rejection. Use these strengths to empower you as you face rejection. Be proud of your accomplishments and qualities. One rejection is nothing compared to several of your strengths, accomplishments, friends, achievements and other positive things in your life.

Take note, there is a fine line between being proud and being arrogant. Remember to build up your humility; often your accomplishments can be credited not only to yourself but also to others who supported you.

Action: Prepare an inventory of your strengths. Start first with a list of positive adjectives that best describe you today. Some qualities are apparent only to people other than you. You may opt to ask them to list them down for you. Some examples of these adjectives are: artistic, kind, unique, active, perceptive, responsive, happy, lovable, responsible, beautiful, creative, confident, supportive or trustworthy. You can use your 2-3 friends that you agreed to mutually support during times of rejection and get their opinion regarding your strengths. That will build your relationships with them and you can also identify their strengths.

Addressing Your Challenges

"Our greatest weakness lies in giving up. The most certain way to succeed is always to try just one more time."

-Thomas Edison

While it takes humility to list down your strengths, it requires courage to list down your challenges. To accurately gauge your needs against rejection, you also have to face your challenges. This will give you an idea of the risk factors that may predispose you to the negative feelings or failures to cope with rejection.

Remember, listing down your challenges is not meant to depress you but to accept them as part of your being. Some challenges you have can be overcome but there are some that are already part of your personality or character. These challenges are still part of you, instead of tripping in life because of them, knowing their existence will allow you to avoid or skip over them.

Challenges are bound to create obstacles for you but instead of letting them defeat you, choose to pick yourself up again and again. Just like Edison, he did not allow the challenges of more than 10,000 mistakes prevent him from finally inventing the light bulb. However, he used each of those mistakes and those challenges to learn from them until he finally reached success. You can do the same for yourself; use your challenges to your advantage. Use the experience of correcting your mistakes caused by your challenges in life as stepping stones towards achieving success.

Action: The same way you listed your strengths, it is now time to list your weaknesses. This part may also require the help of trusted friends in building an accurate profile of your qualities.

Developing a Confident Attitude

"The soul that is within me no man can degrade."

-Frederick Douglass

Rejection may take a toll on your self-confidence but the converse is also true. Self-confidence can tone down the effects of rejection. Developing an overall confident attitude is the culmination of celebrating your strengths and addressing your challenges.

When you are done with a personal assessment of your strengths and challenges, you can start expanding your sources of confidence through your family, friends and other loved ones. Keep them close to you; they will be on your side no matter what. They will know when to support and when to give you space.

As you have a support group to back you up, you should also expect a certain number of individuals who you will meet along the way that will do the opposite. They may constantly reject you; test your coping skills or your level or resilience. These people are already outside your control, it is not within your rights to change them for your sake. The best protection against them is a confident and a persistent attitude.

Action: List down individuals, situations or circumstances that are also the major sources of your rejection. Use empathy to discover the reasons behind their rejection of you. If it is within your control then you have it in you to change their opinions and outlook of you. If it is outside your control then choose not to worry or to be troubled by them. Accept them as they are and rely on yourself and your support group to get you through the rejection that comes from these individuals.

Tony Robbins says that the quality of your answers lie in the quality of your questions. Two very effective questions that you ask during this exercise is, "What's funny about this?" and "What's beautiful about this?" It might be helpful to go back to the breathing exercise before exercising your empathy muscles. It will put you in a more centered state and then you'll access more resources within you to reach higher quality answers. Give it a try and see the blessings that you generate.

Part 2

Rejection Situations & Solutions

Now that you have the techniques and tools needed to overcome rejection, you are more than ready to use them in real world scenarios. The succeeding chapters are all about distinct situations, involving different people, relationships and rejection. As said, rejection does not choose any person, it can happen to anyone and in Part 2, you will see how rejection can also occur across aspects of your life.

The major categories, where rejection can take place, include:

- Dates and relationships

- Family

- Social groups

- College

- Job application

- Work

For dates and relationships, this is the umbrella topic that covers both everything from friendly to romantic relationships. This can be between a love interest, a neighbor or any person whom you want to feel accepted. On the chapter on family, it comes to no surprise that the people who are expected to accept you unconditionally can also reject. In this chapter, situations that include close relatives refusing your requests for favors, reconciliation or other situations are covered. Divorces, abandonment and jealousy are also part of this chapter.

The section on social groups involve clubs, memberships, societies or any other clique of people that you want to either be or feel accepted. There are some groups that you want to be included in that would not welcome you, these are where feelings of rejection occur. These are not necessarily friends, as similar to the chapter on personal relationships, but more like important acquaintances that you desire to create a network.

For young adults, one of the most anticipated but also dreaded situations where rejection can occur is during college applications. This is where the entire future can be decided by either the acceptance or the rejection of a college that you are eyeing. For professionals, job applications are the counterpart. Often both colleges and places of work bring some of the greatest impact when a person is rejected by them.

The chapter on work involves situations that range from a proposal, idea, request, sales pitch or any other work related situation that can involve rejection. This can also involve situations in business where products and services are not accepted. Works of art, crafts and other objects made out of your passion and talents can also be rejected. Sometimes, it is these rejections of things that you have created bring the greatest feelings of despair.

There are many more life situations that involve the risk and occurrence of rejection. The succeeding chapters are only the tip of the iceberg. Perhaps, there is no book that can cover all situations where rejection can happen. However, the purpose for Part 2 of the book is to show you the real and practical application of your lessons on how to overcome rejection. The techniques are not only theories or concepts that will stay only in your mind but also they are tools and techniques that can be used in your life.

While not all of these situations may be applicable to you, there may sections in this succeeding chapter that bear close similarities with your past, present or possible future. You can use these specific scenarios to either help you resolve them as you encounter them or when you feel that you are about to experience them. Another use for these specific scenarios are to help others who are in situations similar to the examples on the chapters.

Chapter Five
Dates & Relationships

Every person has the natural desire to belong and this need is best satisfied when you are able to create, develop and sustain deep relationships with another person, whether a boyfriend, girlfriend, spouse, partner or a companion for life. Having a special someone in your life can be one of the most rewarding feelings you can have. You have someone to rely on, to reciprocate your love and for some, even define their purpose in life.

On the other hand, rejection from these relationships can be one of the most painful feelings that a person can have probably in their entire lifetime. There are different kinds of rejections involving relationships. It can be that of a person trying to be accepted by someone he loves but is rejected. It can be during a relationship and for one reason or another; you break up or drift apart. These are different scenarios and each one will have varying reactions to the rejection. Here are some steps to help you overcome rejection when they happen to you:

- Recognize the stages of rejection in terms of loss

- Steer yourself away from being the victim

- Evaluate your partner's reasons

- Be civil

- Try again

Rejection from your partner feels very similar to loss because you are really losing someone you love. When this happens it is normal that you feel the stages that are similar to that of those people who have lost their loved one either from distance, separation, death or other circumstances. The stages and the feelings that you can expect to encounter are denial, anger, bargaining, depression and acceptance.

During the denial stage, you will not even believe that you were rejected. When you begin to realize that the rejection is happening or already happened, then you will feel anger, either towards yourself, your partner or other people. To salvage the relationship, you will begin to bargain, you will say that you are willing to give up or give way to certain expectations. Sadness or loneliness comes in when you can no longer rebuild the relationship and you begin to feel depressed. Finally, in your solitude, you begin to introspect, heal and then finally accept or in this case overcome the rejection.

Take note that these stages are not necessarily chronological in nature. Depending on your personality, you may skip one stage and gain acceptance sooner compared to other people. You can also merge one stage with another and feel two or more emotions at once. There is no timeframe for these stages; some will be able to go through the process in a few months while some will take years. Some may not even recover from the rejection. Knowing these stages will help you be prepared when you do feel these emotions. You will know that given time, you will heal.

One of the most common responses when rejected by a lover is the feeling of being a victim. You will feel that there is something wrong with you, something unfair has happened to you or the rejection is something that you do not deserve. Again, these are normal feelings to have, especially during the immediate moments after the rejection. However, these feelings become dangerous when they are felt in a prolonged manner. When you are no longer able to live a normal life because of these feelings, you need professional help to overcome it.

While it may be the last thing in your mind, you also need to consider your former partner's reasons why you were rejected. Evaluate the reasons and when deemed true or valid, use them to improve on your social skills and other characteristics. Sometimes, your former partner will not always give you the reason, when this happens avoid putting words in his mouth. Do not attempt to over analyze and put in assumptions.

It may be difficult at first but you can move on sooner when you choose to be civil with your ex partner. The more you distance yourself, the greater the possibility that you retain feelings of contempt, sadness or other negative feelings. Instead, choose to move on by normalizing your relationship with them in a non romantic but still friendly way.

Of course, the best way to overcome rejection from a relationship is to not only move on but also to try again. When you are ready open yourself again to the possibility of love. Never use old experiences from hindering you from growing, seeking new relationships and perhaps even finding the one person that is best for you. Overcoming rejection in relationships is a combination of knowing more about yourself, so you can better yourself for the next relationship.

Chapter Six
Family

One of the supposed bastions of unconditional care, love and acceptance is the family. This is the place where a child grows, a teenager finds his identity and an adult becomes a parent. The family environment makes all of this growth possible because of the power of total acceptance by members of family. The family is a person's refuge, the one place where they can feel that they belong, where they can feel accepted no matter what and the last place where rejection can be expected.

However, the truth is the family situation is one of the earliest situations where a person can feel rejected. As early as childhood and as late as adulthood, rejection can occur. The difficulty with dealing with rejection from the family itself has to do with two things. First is because of the surprise or shock that are felt by those who are caught unaware of the occurrence of rejection in the family.

Second is because rejection, when it occurs in the family especially during the formative years of the rejected person, the tendency is to perpetuate the rejection or to become victimized by it in the long term. Studies prove this tendency. For example, a child who is rejected by a parent will have the tendency to reject their own children when they become parents themselves. When a wife is divorced by her husband, there is a tendency to become hesitant and suspicious of future partners because of previous experiences. There are other scenarios that point out to a vicious cycle caused by rejection.

Some of the most common situations where rejection occurs are between:

- A child rejected by a parent, such as abandonment

- A parent rejected by a child, such as rebellion

- A sibling to another sibling, such as those caused by rivalry

- An adult by another adult, such as divorce or separation

- An entire family branch rejecting an individual or a group, such as being ostracized

Regardless of the individuals involved, rejection in the family can be overcome through the following steps.

- Identifying the rejection cues

- Verbalization of the feeling of rejection

- Finding the causes

- Accepting the situation

- Resolution of the rejection

- Detachment if needed

- Creation of new family

Identifying the rejection cues involve an understanding of the signs of rejection. Take note that rejection can come in different ways and it can be expressed n different manners. In fact, most rejection that occurs in the family does not begin with a verbalized rejection. Before you even hear "No" or "I do not want you," you will receive non verbal messages that may indicate not only impending rejection but also presently being rejected.

For example, if you are a wife and you see that your husband is gradually becoming physically distant from you then this may be an underlying situation of rejection. Sometimes, rejection can be so covert or subtle that it is often mistaken for something else other rejection itself. For example, if you are a child that only receives financial support from your parents and receive little to almost no physical attention or emotional response, then these distances can mean rejection. You need to pay attention to either drastic or a gradual changes in behavior from your family members to determine potential rejection.

When you have these assumptions, the next best thing to do is to confirm if they are true or unfounded. Never let these guesses stay that way, either they are confirmed or not. You cannot live your life with these thoughts. This means you need to verbalize your feeling. Find the courage to ask your family member directly. Do not begin your sentence with an accusatory stance; do not ask "Why are you rejecting me?" Instead, you can verbalize your feelings this way, "I am feeling rejected by your right now, if I am right please let me know." You may discover that there is no rejection to overcome at all.

However, if you do confirm that there is rejection, you need to give yourself time to think of the causes. Is it something you did? Is it something your family member did? Is it a situation within or outside the family? Is it something that you can change? Or your family can change? The most important factor here is to keep the communication lines open. Instead of letting the idea fester between you by keeping it within your thoughts, air it out in the open. Only in this situation can healing start.

While you are finding the causes of the rejection, you need to accept the situation. Nothing good can come from denial and the sooner that you accept that you are being rejected by a member of your family; the sooner can you take steps to overcome it. Denying can also take several forms; there may be instances that you are in denial without even knowing it. For example, you can keep on making excuses for your family's actions to cover the fact that distance is building between you and them.

Once you have gone through these steps, you can begin resolving the causes of the rejection. You can reach out to them, seek or give forgiveness or any other solution that address the main cause of the rejection in the first place. You can start using the techniques shared with you on Part 1 of this book to help you overcome rejection. For example, you can keep positive thoughts to help you go through your situation. You can also seek the help of others, such as other family relatives to help you along the way.

However, you also need to accept that there are certain situations that the cause of the rejection cannot be solved. For you to overcome rejection, you have to let the situation run its course. For example, you may need to detach yourself from your family and your home temporarily. Find another place to stay, go to a relative or a friend. Give you and your family time to reflect. Overcoming rejection may not be done overnight but perhaps, in a few weeks, you will have the time to be by yourself and consider all options.

Your family does not define you but only you can affirm and maintain your self worth. Even if your partner, your family or relatives do not accept you, the first person to accept you is you yourself. When you have considered all options and you have done everything you can but still you are rejected, then it may be time to say goodbye to the family member who rejected you. Find the support of your closest friends or extended family. Remember, you are your own person. In case that the situation does not resolve itself and you are rejected by your own family, then the final task to do is to create your own family.

Chapter Seven
Social Groups

Social groups are another kind of category of relationships where rejection can occur. While rejection from these people may not cause the same amount of anxiety, stress or despair like other relationships, these situations create a different negative impact on you. For example important networks or opportunities are lost when access to these groups is not given. Privileges or perks that you have always dreamed of may not be granted.

There are different situations that can belong to this group:

- Rejection by a club or social organization

- Fraternities, sororities or similar groups

- Professional associations

When these rejections occur, you can use any of these steps to help you overcome it:

- Learn

- Try again

- Seek sponsors

- Move on

Most of these social groups have a strict code for allowing entry. When you experience the first waves of emotions after the rejection, remember to make use of the techniques listed in Part 1. For example, when a country club refuses you membership, then you need to learn from the rejection. Do your research and find the reason behind the rejection.

Was it because you did not meet a certain standard? Is there anything that you can do to reach this standard? How do other members behave? How can you adjust? Seek out the principles and core beliefs that the social group has. Find out how you can meet these values so you can better fit into their group.

When you have done your research and you have learned from your lessons, the next step is to try again. Identify the ways that the groups will allow for a second try or a second chance. When you have this information, grab and use them. Take full advantage of your previous experience of rejection and use it to propel you towards success on this try. Remember that rejection does not necessarily mean the end of your journey towards gaining acceptance; it can be the opportunity for something else.

One of the most important factors that can help you not only overcome but also maybe reverse rejection from social groups is through seeking sponsors. Sometimes even with careful research and use of previous experience, having the guidance of a current member will increase your chances for acceptance. Knowing who is who in the group, gaining access to information made only available to members and other tips that can help you gain entry and succeed on your second try can be received from a sponsor. Of course, if are able to convince this sponsor to voice out their support of you, this public support will go far.

There are also instances that no effort you use will bring you acceptance to your chosen group. When this happens, it is best to seek alternatives to the group. Find another group that can still provide you with the same or closest to same benefits that your target group can provide. Move on and do not let the rejection from this group derail you from the chance to become a member of another one. It may seem that you are choosing a lesser alternative, do not let this thought prevail in your mind. It will not do you any good, instead use a positive outlook and believe that this group may have rejected you because a better group is better for you.

Before you even begin on this track of doing everything you can to belong to a group it is important that you first make a personal review. Do you need to adjust at all? Do you have to change yourself to meet their standards? In the first place, do you need to be a member of this group entirely? Sometimes in the course of trying to gain acceptance from these groups, you lose track of your identity. You begin to sacrifice too much of yourself. You may also use up too much of your resources in your quest to gain acceptance. You need to make a conscious decision to arrive at a balance between your decision of trying for acceptance or overcoming rejection by moving on.

Chapter Eight
College

College is a rite of a passage for most people, being accepted to one brings great joy and satisfaction to those who applied. Being accepted also gives them a sense of achievement and direction for their future. However, the same level of joy that is felt when a person is accepted can also be the same level of anxiety felt when a person is rejected. For a young adult with his entire life in front of him to be suddenly stopped in its track by a letter of rejection from a college can really cause anxiety.

Handling rejection from the colleges that you have applied for can be done in different techniques that build on your awareness of the reasons behind rejections or even the chance to seek for reconsideration. Some of these are:

- Knowing college profiles

- Expanding options

- Handling humiliation

- Letting it run its course

When an applicant is rejected, several factors contributed to the rejection and some of these reasons do not necessarily reflect on the character of the applicant. Colleges have their own distinct personality which influences their decision on whether to accept or reject applicants.

For example, a university known for its standard for overachievers and highly active student population will prefer one applicant over another when compared to an applicant who is more laid back. A college that focuses on the sciences will prefer another applicant compared to a college that looks for those with a passion for the arts. This means that sometimes when you are rejected from a college, it does not mean that you failed but that you are a better fit somewhere.

This means that you have to expand your options. Rejection from one college does not necessarily mean rejection from all other colleges out there. Be more open to other educational institutions, have more than one option for your college education, take three, five or more. Choose Ivy League institutions, state and community colleges. When you fail in one, have another three that you can take.

One of the first worries of those who were rejected is the peer pressure or the shame from being rejected. College applicants often lodge their application in groups, like with other classmates. When one person fails, chances are everybody else will know that he has failed. Give yourself the courage to ignore these feelings of shame and use it instead to boost your efforts in finding the right college for you.

While you can prepare yourself for the rejection, there will always be the mild to severe case of anxiety when you receive the dreaded rejection letter. When this happens, it will be normal to feel these emotions, do not suppress them. Instead let these feelings run through you and let the feelings run its course. You will feel bad, worried or afraid but when you have allowed yourself to feel these and share it with others like your family or friends you will feel a lot better than when you keep it yourself.

Another course you can take when trying to overcome rejection from your college application is to consider other options aside from college. College is truly an important part of building your career but it is not the only path available to you. Building a business of your own, pursuing your talents and other opportunities are still available to those who have not graduated from college. Being rejected by colleges is not the end of the world but it can be another door opening for you.

Chapter Nine
Job Application

Similar to college application, job applications also cause the same degree of anxiety when encountered by young professionals ready for their first job or for their next career move. The reason why rejection from job applications can be so worrisome is because of the immense expectations on that job application. Fresh from the university, a student will still have idealized thoughts on his chances towards employment. He may feel that after all his hard work in college; he will be rewarded by a slot in his target company.

However, chances are, things will not always go your way during job applications. You realize that you are not the only applicant. You will not always have the best credentials and some will even have better qualifications done you. When this happens, you may get rejected from your first, second or even third option.

Handling job rejections requires not only approaching it in the right perspective but also in the right set of strategies. You have to use more than stress management, positive thinking or other techniques. You have to use these techniques simultaneously with job hunting specific strategies that will increase your chances of getting the job that you want. Nothing will help you overcome rejection from job applications than getting the job itself.

Some of these strategies are:

- Make a unique resumé

- Have a great interview

- Customize your application

Sometimes, it is not a lack of qualifications that result from your rejection but a failure to package yourself in the best possible way. Remember, job applications are all about selling yourself, your talents and your achievements to your prospective employer. Your first impression in the company is made via your resumé. Do you research and find the best practices and trends in making this document. For example, if you are a graphic artist, add a link to your portfolio instead of a text only document. If you are a sales professional, list down your achievements in terms of actual money figures.

Your next challenge is your interview. Your resumé can only get you as far as the job interview. Do not let the memories of your previous job rejection feel you less confident. Instead use those experiences as your tips on how to succeed on the next interview. Learn from previous mistakes if there were any and apply those lessons in your next interactions with your panel of interviewers.

One way to increase your chances of getting accepted by a company is to customize your application to their company. For example, find out their vision or mission statements and find their list of company values. Subtly incorporate these words into your answers or documents. Aside from their history, look into their current projects and use specific examples of how you can contribute directly to these new projects or activities.

Rejection from job applications are best overcome in the short term by using the techniques on Part 1 of this book but for long term relief, nothing beats being employed to help you move on.

Chapter Ten

Work

You may have found yourself accepted into a job but do not think that everything will be smooth sailing from here on. In fact, you will be probably encountering more rejections than you have ever before. Handling rejection at work requires you to become more than mature enough to accept it but also professional enough to overcome it.

Work related rejection can come in many forms:

- Not being promoted for a position that you are aiming for

- Not invited to a posse within your company that you want to belong in

- Not getting a project or assignment that is attractive

- Failed business transaction

- Rejection of a proposal or ideas

Here are some strategies to help you overcome rejection in your role as a professional:

- Bring yourself back to pre-rejection status

- Ask and use feedback

- Expose yourself to the right people

Immediately after the rejection, expect feelings of disappointment, anger or even loss of confidence. These are normal but do not let these emotions fester. Instead, make sure that you bring yourself back to the pre-rejection status. This is needed because as long as you have those negative emotions with you, you will not be able to bring out the best output that you can really make. These will only act as obstacles towards your achievement.

Instead of only accepting feedback, actively search and request for it. Every bit of idea that you can gather are steps toward your improvement. These improvements in turn will bring you closer toward receiving the professional acceptance that you are aiming for.

The traditional view of gaining professional acceptance is through sheer hard work and exemplary performance. Once, it is believed that the better you perform, the greater you chances of being accepted to that position you want or the project that you want to involve yourself in. However, there is a new thinking now being taught among professional circles, especially among career development experts.

This new idea says that your performance can contribute only to as low as 10% of your chances for acceptance. The rest is about exposing yourself to the right people. This means that your performance, however great it is, will be useless when they remain unknown by the people who make the decisions on your career. For example, you may have signed a big deal which brought in a huge revenue. Still, if these sales figures are only added with your group's total contribution to revenue, then you may not be credited or recognized for the success.

Make sure that your performance is known not only by your immediate supervisor but also with the movers and shakers of your company. Also, take into account not only those who belong to your unit or department but also the rest of the office employees. You will need sponsors both from staff, peers and superiors to gain the acceptance that you want.

Part 3
Advanced Techniques

Part 1 and 2 of this book was all about the technique to help you overcome rejection after it has occurred. Part 3 helps you overcome rejection in a different timeframe. This is through preparing yourself so that you may not need to overcome rejection at all because you will increase your chances of being accepted.

Chapter Eleven
Preparing for No

Overcoming rejection does not only require techniques that can be used after the rejection has occurred. To help you overcome rejection, you need to prepare yourself even before it occurs. Preparing for the "No" is all about making plans just in case you are rejected. The better you plan for the potential of rejection, the better you can overcome it when it does happen.

Preparing for rejection includes setting up contingencies, Plan Bs and other options that can help you bounce back after rejection occurs. When you have these options place, the blow of rejection is softened. If you are a student eyeing for your dream college, do not put all your eggs or in this case college application into one basket, you need to cover as many colleges as you can. This way when you are rejected for one college, you have other universities on standby that will potentially accept you.

If you are planning to make a sales target then you need to cover all scenarios. Find more than one prospective customer or client. If you are dating, then make yourself available and meet as many people as you can instead of looking for one ideal person. If you want to belong to a social group, find other groups that can offer you the same benefits as with your intended group.

Also, simulate the situation where you are rejected. What emotions will you feel? What changes in your lifestyle will occur? What will be your immediate reactions? What resources will you lose? When you take into account these situations, you can prepare yourself so that you are not surprised by the circumstances after the rejection occurs. When you are armed with these plans and when you prepare yourself for these situations, you will be even less anxious about the situation. Knowing that you are prepared, you will feel at ease during the situations, which in turn increases the chances for your success.

Take note that planning in advance does not guarantee that you will never get the No. However, planning does more than prepare you for the potential rejection but it will give you a certain degree of peace mind that can lessen the stress.

Chapter Twelve
Anticipating the Yes

While it is important that you plan for the worst, you must always balance yourself with optimism. This is where the concept of faking it till you make it becomes applicable. This concept states that you need to visualize yourself in your moment of success. The same set of questions that you ask yourself when you are planning for the No, such as how would you look like, how would you act, how would you speak and other questions can be asked.

Now start acting on these visualized cues. Dress the part, act the part and be the part of a person who is accepted instead of someone who is rejected. Keep behaving in such a way that you are faking it, as if you have already been accepted. Your future accepted self will soon merge with your current self. You will find yourself not pretending or faking it anymore but you actually become the person who is accepted.

When you have this confident demeanor of being accepted, from something as simple in the way you talk, speak and behave and to the thoughts that you have and the decisions you make, all of these things will be exuded. The people, whom you want to receive acceptance from, will notice these changes in you. They will see in you the traits, characteristics and demeanor of someone who they want. When they do begin to deliberate whether to accept or reject you, your positive actions will influence them towards deciding in your favor.

For example, when you are trying to impress someone, do not approach them as if you are trying to feel accepted. Do not look needy or desperate; instead present yourself in the complete opposite. Show yourself as someone who has been accepted. Your confidence will bring you real success and acceptance.

By anticipating the Yes, you create within you the persona of someone who is accepted, except for a psyche of someone who is rejected. This is a very important principle that you can use even when you are rejected. You will know that even after you are rejected, you have the resources within you to become accepted, maybe not now but certainly in the future.

John Baskin

Chapter Thirteen
Fear of Rejection

One of the most crippling fears that can lead to rejection or prevent you from overcoming rejection is the fear of rejection itself. It is important to note that the fear of rejection is not something to be ashamed of. If you have this fear, then take solace that you are not the only one who has this fear. In fact, the fear of rejection is not only widespread but also can be traced far back into human history.

The fear of rejection is said to come from the human instinct that comes from the need to belong. During ancient times, when people lived together as a tribe or as a member of a community, the need to belong is strong. This is because during those times, one cannot afford to be excluded, People needed each other to live, one cannot survive on their own because of the dangers of wildlife or even other tribes. When one is excluded from the tribe,

80

they open themselves to the dangers of those who do not belong or those who are not accepted.

The same instinct persists until now. Even during the modern times, the need to belong is just as strong as it was thousands of years ago. Instead of tribes and means of survival, there are now groups both real and virtual and employment, businesses and other means of living. People around the world, regardless of age, gender, race or any other background in life will have this fear. The only difference is how they use this fear of rejection.

There are two ways that people allow the fear to affect them. First there are those who allow the fear to affect them negatively. Some are so fearful of rejection that their growth is stunted. Forever wanting to be safe, they stay within their comfort zones. They keep only the company of those who accepts them and they are too afraid to consider other relationships that may open them for growth but still pose the risk for rejection. Living this life of constant fear will not bring you anywhere. It will keep you from growing into the person that you are meant to be. Plus, the fear will never go away but it will fester in your psyche until it becomes part of your outlook in life.

On the other hand, there are those who use this fear in a positive way. When there is a fear, people will use it to propel themselves toward better performance, better relationships and better outlook in life. Instead of fear, it becomes a sort of anxiety that can trigger you to becoming a better person. Knowing that there is a potential for rejection, you will push yourself towards doing the best that you can. To avoid the rejection or to get rid of the anxiety of rejection, you create ways to make sure that it never happens. People who use anxiety, not as a crutch, but as a stepping stone towards progress are useful.

Remember, the fear of rejection is not something bad; it is natural and sometimes necessary to help you grow. It becomes good when you are able to use it to reach your full potential by challenging you beyond your limits. On the other hand and when you are not able to use it in the proper way, it can become an obstacle that will only stunt your growth.

Chapter Fourteen
Self-Approval

One of the most important principles that you can live by when you are dealing with rejection is the concept of self approval. While acceptance and belongingness are truly needed in life, it is by no means that only thing in life. Overcoming rejection too is important but only to the limit that you do not resort to a chronic need for approval.

Called approval seeking behaviors, these are actions that you have to watch out for. The more you use them, the closer you are to becoming dependent on others for your self-worth and value instead of yourself. There are many manifestations of the need to receive constant approval from others.

Some of them are:

- Always doing something you are not expected or required to do, just because you do not want to say No yourself.

- Letting go of certain actions made against you, thinking that if you confront them you will lose their approval

- Agreeing to ideas, discussions or things that you do not really agree with just to keep the relationship intact

- Feeling anxiety, worry or anger when you are disagreed with

- Constantly being apologetic even when not needed

- Showing that you know more than you really do fearing that you will be disapproved when the extent of your knowledge is uncovered

- Spreading rumors or facts that demean or degrade others so that they reject others but you are uplifted or accepted in return

- Striving to conform or to be accepted by changing your identity, values, beliefs or any other personal characteristics

There are many more behaviors that can point out a person who strives to be accepted at the expense of everything else about himself. You need to look at yourself or ask for the observation of other people to gauge if you have these behaviors and if they are pointing to an approval seeking tendencies.

If you do have these tendencies, then you need to take steps to get rid of these behaviors by replacing them with self acceptance or self approval. There are many steps that you can take to achieve these outlooks in life:

Begin by asking yourself simple but very important questions. These questions can be answered at the privacy of your own home or deep in your thoughts, try to answer them as honestly as you can: Do you accept yourself? Do you need external approval to make you feel good about yourself? Do you judge yourself and if so, how do you judge?

When you realize that you a low sense of self acceptance, then you need to change. Begin letting go of the thought that you need approval from others and that you should begin to by approving yourself first. Start by feeling good about yourself, celebrate your strengths and accomplishments. Recall the moments when you have stood your ground, stayed honest about yourself and accepted yourself. Feel how empowering those moments were and draw from them in your quest for self acceptance.

Make a conscious effort to watch yourself for the behaviors that point to seeking approval. Also, ask the support of your friends to help you with the observation. At any time that you see yourself doing it, replace it immediately with words of self affirmation.

Take note that this period of adjustment do not happen overnight. When you have made a habit out of these behaviors, it will take time before you will be able to get rid of it. However, there is no time to procrastinate, the sooner you start checking yourself and unlearning these behaviors, the sooner you will free yourself from it.

Chapter Fifteen
Negotiation & Standing Your Ground

Negotiation is a technique that is used when you are in the situation of being rejected. When you feel that there is still an opportunity to be accepted or there is still room to make your case for approval, then negotiation is one of the best techniques that you can use. Whether you are a couple trying to mend their relationship together, you are an employee trying to ask support from your boss or you are a salesperson trying to seal the deal, negotiation can mean the difference between acceptance and rejection.

Different negotiation techniques are available and appropriate for every rejection scenario. However, most of these techniques share the same general principles. Some negotiations steps that you need to learn are:

- Knowing your value

- Taking it slow

- Planning the tactic

- Showing proof

- Giving and taking

Before you go into any negotiation to receive acceptance, you need to know the value of what you are offering. If you are seeking acceptance of a product or service, then you need to know everything about what you are selling, not only its benefits or pros but also its risks and cons. Take the negotiation slowly, nothing good will come out of rushing. Give yourself time to prepare or plan. During negotiation, pace yourself so that you have time to think and listen to what the other party is saying.

At the same time, it is important to plan a tactic that is suited to the profile of the other person. Do not use the cookie cutter approach in negotiation, find the pressure points of the other person, what does he want that you have, what is his personality or what are the things that he values the most. When you have this profile, you can customize your approach to make the negotiation more effective. Bring along with you any proof that will support your claims for grounds for reconsideration or acceptance.

Remember, negotiation is not always about you taking something from another party. Every relationship involves one form of give and take. You need to offer something in return for the acceptance that you want. At the same time, give yourself a limit on what you can and should give.

Another technique that you can use during rejection is to stand your ground. This is when you remain firm, confident and refuse to take No for an answer. When you are truly confident of your worth, validity of your idea and other definite factors that necessitate acceptance, then you have every right to persist.

Part 4
Special Topics

Chapter Sixteen
Across Ages & Genders

Rejection may be a universal phenomenon but each person experiences and reacts to it in their unique way. However, certain patterns exist on the type of reaction to rejection that can be linked to an age-related factor. Major age groups, reflected by their level of maturity and emotional status, have a huge influence on how persons react to rejection.

These differences are important to note because the more you know how your peers in your age group react, the better you can overcome it. Also aside from being aware of your own circumstances, you can also make use of these ideas on age related differences towards other people.

One pattern that is supported by research is that as a person ages, the greater the anxiety over rejection is felt. This means younger people are able to bounce again from rejection in easier ways compared to older people who have a harder time in overcoming rejection. For example, a study done that compared the levels of hurt felt by those ages from 18 to 26 and those from ages 60 and above. The senior members of the research reported being hurt in greater levels compared to the junior participants.

Children

During childhood years, the sources of rejection are primarily found in schools and among groups of friends, neighborhood posses and sport team and other similar cliques. If you are a parent, older sibling or any other adult that is responsible for the welfare of the child, then you need to know the concepts behind rejection during childhood.

The first step you need to take is to prepare yourself for the rejection of the child. Adults have the tendency to react to rejection from their children or other young people based on their own experience in the past. As a result, they may unconsciously share the same coping mechanisms they used when they children themselves. The risk in this method is that you preempt the child from discovering his own way in dealing with rejection. Also, the environment where you were rejected is very different from today. For example, a parent will have difficulty providing advice to a child rejected in the virtual world, such as through social media, when she has not yet encountered the same kind of rejection.

It is important that when you help a child overcome rejection that you do so from an emphatic standpoint. Being rejected by a club at school may seem unimportant to adults but for a child, the rejection can be one of the most hurtful things that he thinks he will encounter in his life. When this happens, listen to the child and make sure to take note that whatever he says is important is truly important in him in a subjective standpoint. Do not belittle the rejection and dedicate the same effort as you would any other kind of rejection.

Also, when you help the child to cope, give him the chance to develop his own steps, techniques or strategies to overcome the rejection. Spoon feeding the child to overcome rejection will definitely be easier but only in the short term. As much as possible, try to guide your child into equipping himself with the tools to overcome rejection by himself so that we have grows up, he has childhood experiences that can help him cope.

Due to their lack of experience, children will still have an idealized version of the reality around them. If they believe that they are good in sports, then they may think that they can get into the team. Be very wary when dealing with children, you must manage their expectations especially if you see that they are really passionate on an activity. Ground them into reality and use it to help them work harder to get into the team or the group.

Teenagers

The next major age group that brings about probably the most tumultuous years in a person's life is those that belong to teenagers. Changes in their body and in their psyche, especially the need for identity formation, bring about the greatest need for belongingness. When a teenager finds a group to belong to, much of teenage anxiety is decreased. However when any form of rejection takes place, it causes an equally great anxiety that is felt.

If you are a teenager or you want to help a teenager overcome rejection, you need a separate set of tools. For example, meditation, stress management and verbalization of feelings may be effective for other age groups or situations but for teenagers they may be either ineffective or even harmful. This is because teenagers thrive on the concept of independence. They prefer to do things on their own way and without the support of adults. As a result of showing that they can do it on their own, they can refuse your help or ignore it altogether.

You need to customize your approach to teenagers who are rejected. Some of the techniques that you can use are:

Give them space

- Be patient

- Watch out for risky behavior

Keep yourself available and ready to listen to teenagers. However, do not look over their shoulders constantly instead give them space. Remember, they thrive on being able to do things themselves. Give them the opportunity to learn from their mistakes and the rejection. For teenagers there is a thin line between you helping and you intruding. When they are ready, teenagers will approach and ask for your help. However, always remind them that you are there and ready to listen to them when they are ready to talk.

Characterized by outbursts and rebelliousness, you need all the patience you can muster to help teenagers overcome rejection. There will long periods of crying, isolation, refusal to communication, tempers and other mood swings that will test your patience. When this happens, keep yourself composed. If you need to vent out frustration, do it outside your home so that the teenager is not affected.

While maintaining distance is good, you also need to be very vigilant of risky behavior. Teenagers with their outbursts and erratic behavior have the tendency to manifest their anxiety and other emotions into physically destructive behavior. Keep an eye for those who are staying out too late in the evening, those who are becoming more and more reclusive or detached from other people.

One of the most important factors that you have to look into is any physical changes in their bodies. For example, rejection can be very painful and one way to relieve the anxiety felt from it is through manifesting it in physically harmful behavior. This way the pain from the rejection is temporarily replaced or covered by the physical pain. Physical changes can mean anything from weight chances, self inflicted wounds, drug abuse and other destructive behavior.

Take note that these behaviors must be addressed not only by themselves but also by their root cause, which is the rejection itself. While you can treat the diet change or wounds, you have to address the greater issue to resolve all issues once and for all.

It does not mean that adults, who have already matured and gained the knowledge and wisdom from years of experience, will be able to cope and overcome rejection easily when compared to those younger than them. While Part 1 and 2 of this book are geared towards the use of adults, another step may also be necessary for them.

Professional Support

Beyond the social support of family, friends and loved ones, overcoming rejection can be emotionally taxing that disturbances in the psyche becomes the result. When this occurs, professional support is needed. Life coaches, doctors, therapists and other professions are needed to provide adults and even other ages the scientifically based treatment required.

Reactions to rejection also differ based on the sex and gender of the person. Studies show that women have increased hormonal responses when rejected; this means that there is added anxiety felt by women compared to men. However, aside from this research, there is not much scientific research that shows a significant difference between overcoming rejection among males and females. Most discussions are anecdotal in nature.

Chapter Seventeen
Famous People who were Rejected

Another way to help you overcome rejection is to be inspired by the many success stories of people who have surpassed the anxiety and difficulties of rejection. These persons are made famous by their great achievements and acceptance by the groups they belong to and the world they live in. They come from all walks of life, backgrounds, industries and even time.

Anna Wintour

Arguably the most powerful woman in fashion, Anna Wintour is the Editor in Chief of American Vogue. Under her leadership, the magazine has gained unprecedented levels of success. So great were her achievements that she has been named Creative Director of the entire publishing house. Her opinions and company are sought after by fashion designers, celebrities, magnates and political figures.

For her many achievements, not only in the fashion but also political and philanthropic circles, she has received numerous accolades including knighthood from Great Britain.

It may be surprising that she traces her success not only from a series of accomplishments but also of failures. She is often quoted as saying that, "I recommend that you all get fired. It's a great learning experience." Anna was fired in her position as Junior Editor. If she has given up on that rejection, she would not have reached the level of success that she is enjoying right now.

One lesson that can be learned from Anna is an unflappable belief in herself. She knows her value as a person and as a professional. She carried with her a confidence that people around her cannot help but feel attracted to and feel valuable. When you are seeking acceptance from others, remember to remain confident and believing in yourself.

Steve Jobs

Being fired in your job is bad but being fired from your own company can be worse. The late Steve Jobs is one of the most innovative and creative minds of the modern world. Under his direction, Apple, the company has revolutionized phones, laptops and computers and now more new devices. The company is now one the highest valued company in the world with annual revenues higher than even the GDP of entire countries.

Although he is well known as the CEO of Apple, there was a point in his career where he was removed from his own company. Instead of wallowing from depression or lashing out of anger, he used his energy to create an entirely new company, Pixar. This company went on to creating some of the most famous animated movies, such as Toy Story, Finding Nemo, Inside Out and the very popular Frozen and Minions.

Upon his triumphant return to Apple, Steve brought the company to even greater heights and success. His designs, his drive and his passion are all reflected in the devices that have become widely accepted in the globe. One of lesson in overcoming rejection from Steve is that he thrived on self acceptance and not social acceptance. He is often quoted as saying that Apple does not do market research. Instead, he knows what the people wants before they even know they want it. If Steve was entirely dependent on what customers wanted from his designs, the Apple products may not be as successful as they are now.

Steven Spielberg

Winning 11 Emmy's 7 Globes and 3 Oscars, Steven Spielberg may be the most well known director of Hollywood and perhaps even the world. Under his direction, some of the movies that he has been involved in various capacities include: Close Encounters of the Third Kind, Saving Private Ryan, Jaws, Jurassic Park, AI and the Indiana Jones series. His name is often equated with not only thought provoking artistry in the film genre but also of profitability, commercial success and worldwide acceptance.

Before he was the successful director that he is now, he once applied to the University of Southern California School of Theatre, Film and Television. He was rejected 3 times. Imagine someone as great as Steven being rejected by a film school. Average young adults who are applying for colleges may feel defeated or even refuse to try again. Steven did not only try again, he did so for three times. This is a testament to another lesson that can be learned from these once rejected but now successful people.

Tenacity and persistence are important to overcome rejection. They are the attitudes you need to help you carry yourself up when you fall because of rejection. However, the same way that persistence is important, you also need to know when to move on. Steven did try to apply but he was rejected and instead he chose to apply to another college, there he was accepted.

Sometimes, you need to take a moment, breathe and consider all your options. Tenacity is commendable but when misplaced, it will only hinder you from success instead of bring you closer to it. Learn to be flexible and adjust as needed. Consider all opportunities instead of being locked into a few choices. Your first choice may reject you but the choice that is best for you may accept you after all.

Oprah Winfrey

Media mogul, philanthropist, recipient of the Presidential Medal of Freedom, holder of doctorate degrees and the richest black billionaire in the U.S., Oprah Winfrey is another person that you can take inspiration from. Her life is one of the best examples of rags to riches story. She was into a poor family and experienced several traumatic incidents on her life. From being raped at the age of nine to giving birth to a child at age fourteen.

Despite these difficulties, she climbed the ranks from being a journalist, to a report, to the host of her own show. Soon, her media empire grew and she found acceptance in every home through her shows. Her opinions mattered, her endorsements were accepted and her entire lifestyle was emulated. However, despite the success, Oprah still had challenges.

One of the most publicized challenges that she encountered was her weight. The public saw how her weight seesawed from being overweight, to being fit then back to gaining the weight she lost.

However, instead of resorting to self rejection, she took an entirely different stance. She faced this issue head on, instead of hiding from it.

This is an important lesson to learn in overcoming rejection. You need to know your worth as a person and not equate it with your weight and when challenges does occur, when you are in danger of being rejected by either yourself or others, you need to accept it as really happening. Nothing good can come from denying what is the truth. The more you ignore it, the longer it will take you to recover from it or in this case overcome rejection. You do not need to go out in public and show your challenges to the world; instead you can begin by accepting it yourself and then working on resolving the rejection and moving on.

Albert Einstein

His parents report that he was unable to speak until he was four years old and failed to read until he was seven. He was expelled from school too. One could not imagine that the child in this story is Albert Einstein himself. His name, often equated with intelligence and invention, is almost never associated with failure or intellectual delay. However, these are the facts behind Albert's story.

Patience is the lesson that can be learned from Albert. Acceptance does not happen when you want or when it is expected. Sometimes rejection will catch you by surprise and will leave you in shock. Acceptance may not even happen within several months to a few years. Sometimes, even if you do all the techniques for overcoming rejection, this does not guarantee acceptance.

The best that you can do is not to wait for acceptance to happen but you need to be tireless in working towards reaching your goal. Rejection will be there along the way, sometimes few or sometimes many. However, do not be discouraged or fearful of rejection. Instead use it to boost your performance.

Chapter Eighteen
Rejecting Others

Part of learning how to overcoming rejection is to learn how to reject others. This is a lesson on empathy and paying it forward, you also need to know how to properly do a rejection so that other people will have a more positive outlook of rejection. One factor that greatly affects the process of overcoming rejection is the way the rejection was delivered.

Rejection can be embarrassing; it can make people lose their confidence, positivity and even hope. It can cause you pain both in the short and long term. However all of these anxiety and negativities can be reduced when a rejection is delivered properly and with all the courtesies need to soften the blow. While it is the person you are rejecting that can greatly benefit from the way you deliver the rejection, you too will gain some rewards from it.

To reject others, here are some techniques:

Avoid speaking in an emotional, angry or distressed tone, instead be calm, clear and to the point when you are rejecting. People have a tendency to mimic the way people will talk to them, if you take an angry stance when you reject, you will most likely receive the same.

Use a specific set of body language. Avoid showing discomfort or anxiety, such as when you twitch, fidget or eye looking at several directions. Instead, stand straight and do not hunch your back. Put your arms on your sides but not wrapped around your chest. Look at the person straight in the eye.

You can start or add in a sentence the words, "I'm sorry" or "I apologize." This is done more out courtesy so use these words sparingly. Do not apologize too much because when you do the person will think that you are feeling regretful and there is a possibility that your mind can be changed. Construct sentences as simple as you can, do not add any more words than necessary. The shorter the rejection is, the faster you can get out of that situation.

It is acceptable to offer some form of explanation why you are rejecting the person. Do it as briefly as you can. State facts and do not lie. Do not also sugarcoat because it will only be demeaning to the person. Be as honest as you can and do not make excuses for your actions.

One way you can lessen the blow further is to help the other person with moving on from the rejection itself. Instead of just giving the rejection, provide other ways or opportunities where he can be accepted. For example, if you reject the proposal of your staff, offer constructive criticism instead of just saying "No." These steps are mutually beneficial for you and the other person because you can receive better quality work on the next try.

Also, be open to second chances. Do not limit yourself by being biased against people, whom you have rejected. This is not only bad for the other person but also possibly yourself because you may not gain access to advantages when you have accepted the other person.

Whenever a person you have rejected tries again to receive your acceptance, approach it with a fresh set of eyes. You can definitely take into account the previous try of being accepted but do so from an evaluating point of view. Do not use the first rejection against the other person but use it to compare how far he has changed or improved and let those be the measure of your criteria for acceptance.

Part 5

Designing the Lifestyle

Watch your thoughts, they become words.
Watch your words, they become actions.
Watch your actions, they become habits.
Watch your habits, they become your character.
Watch your character, it becomes your destiny.

Although the source of these words is still unknown, this quote is often used as the road map to turn thoughts all the way to becoming habits and shaping your character. There is a wide gap between information about your character and character building. This quote will help you to sustain the steps you learned from this book.

Personalizing the Steps

Browse back through the major steps in this book. Instead of just reading *Transformation into an Opportunity*, rephrase it into a personalized statement. "I will transform every rejection or setback into an opportunity or chance for improvement." Instead of just reading *Coping Immediately* turn it into "I will immediately and powerfully face rejection." Do this for the rest of the major chapter and subchapters titles. List or write down these statements and post them somewhere conspicuous for you to see.

Now turn your words into actions. For every personalized statement, prepare a corresponding action plan. For example, in "I will transform every rejection or setback into an opportunity or chance for improvement," target one memory of a rejection a week. Find out what you have learned or gained due to the rejection. Start with few or easy to achieve targets, success of repetition here is important. You can use those two questions from the previous exercise: "What is funny about this so-called rejection?" and "What is beautiful about this so-called rejection?"

Creating Habits

As you repeat these action plans, you will find yourself doing it almost automatically, as if by second nature. Soon these repetitions become part of your habits; these are other resources that you can draw from should rejections challenge you.

Remember, knowledge is useless if it remains locked in your mind. Express it through your actions and behaviors. The physical manifestation of the knowledge you gained and the lessons you learned are the best testaments to your growth and maturity.

Reaching Your Destiny

When you have turned knowledge into habit and then habit into character, then you are steadily reaching redefining your character into a form that best suits your destiny. Remember, it is never too late to change your personality or character, you can always add coping skills and resilience as part of your being. You may soon see and accept that rejection is a part and not an obstacle to life. In fact, you can use it to tap your potential, become the best version of yourself and bring you closer to your destiny.

What's Next?

To help you in your journey towards overcoming rejection, here are a few more steps to create a concrete action plan. Remember all the previous Action instructions in the end of every subsection? Those are bits and pieces that when put together will make a complete plan for you.

Use a standard letter size blank sheet of paper. On the far right of the paper, write down the SMART vision of yourself, your purpose or passion in life. On the far left side of the paper, write down your recollections of the triggers or circumstances that similarly appear during your rejections. You should have a wide blank space in the middle by this time.

Now on this empty space in the middle, make a horizontal line of words of your strengths. Now take your list of weaknesses, find the appropriate strength that you have that can resolve this weakness. If you used up all your strengths to match, add your list of friends and physical exercises that can match with the weaknesses. If you still have some weaknesses left over, make a vertical line of words in the middle of the paper.

Now it is time to look at your completed work and see what each part symbolizes. This is your roadmap towards reaching your vision. The far right side of your paper represents the completion of your journey or the achievement of your destiny. On the far left side, these are current situations that represent rejection and failures. Bridging the gap is the horizontal line of your strengths, which will lead you to that vision. However, the vertical line is the barrier of weaknesses that prevent you from reaching your destiny.

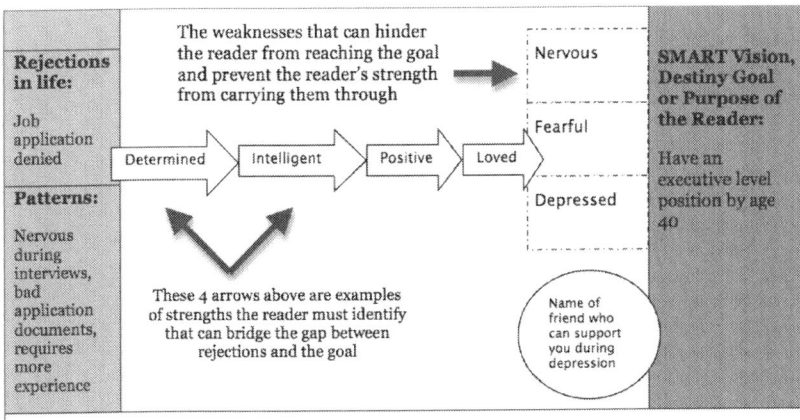

Rejections in life:	The weaknesses that can hinder the reader from reaching the goal and prevent the reader's strength from carrying them through	Nervous	SMART Vision, Destiny Goal or Purpose of the Reader:
Job application denied	Determined → Intelligent → Positive → Loved	Fearful	Have an executive level position by age 40
Patterns: Nervous during interviews, bad application documents, requires more experience	These 4 arrows above are examples of strengths the reader must identify that can bridge the gap between rejections and the goal	Depressed Name of friend who can support you during depression	

How does your road map look like? Did your strengths allow you to reach the far right side of the map? Have you successfully paired every weakness, which is why there is no more vertical barrier?

If your strengths did not reach the vision then you will likely need to develop more attitudes, learn new skills or gather more knowledge. Overcoming rejection is only one of the many self-help topics that can bridge the gap. If you have several lines of weakness barriers then you probably need more time, more support and more effort towards addressing these challenges. Whatever the result of your road map, you may either be disheartened or encouraged, but it is a necessary step towards self-discovery and finding your location on your journey in life. Knowing where you are, where you have been and where you are going are the elements that will bring you closer to the life you deserve to live.

Overcoming rejection can be a difficult endeavor for you. Do not be overwhelmed by this journey, start with the two simple steps: cope with it and build resilience against it. This book can only go as far as giving you the knowledge and techniques on how to make the first two steps. After that, experience will take the place of this book and serve as your teacher. But when your memory fails and you cannot seem to remember how to make a Johari window, then you can always come back and re-read the jewels inside this book. We must have a cognitive understanding of these concepts before we can internalize it emotionally and physically, so that we face situations in spite of fear because we know in our hearts that it will positively serve us. We are here to become more resilient and experience awaits.

Conclusion

I would like to extend thanks out to you once again for downloading this book.

I sure do hope that this book provides more access to overcoming this clouded fear of rejection in your life and that it will be referred to in the future when other challenges are met. But my intention is that with enough persistent application of these jewels, your new associations will be so consciously grounded that you won't feel the need to come back. But, until that time is manifested, may this book serve as your companion in times of egotistical second-guessing.

You already have within you all the resources needed to tackle this disempowering embedded idea of rejection, and it is achieved by taking ownership of your decisions and accessing your personal power.

But, perhaps, you read this book all the way through without taking a breath and it may ignite a temporary high of inspiration, but I will emphasize that the point is not to spark something so shortsighted. That dies because the foundation has not been laid down. We are carving out a mentality in this book where the words become embodied in your body, mind, and spirit. There's a clear distinction between wisdom through knowledge and virtue by application.

With that in mind, the next move is to go back to the beginning and read the first chapter, then complete the challenge at the end of the first chapter before moving on to the next chapter. This is where all the treasure lies.

May we build a strong foundation leading to higher success and fulfillment. The power lies in our decision at any moment.

John Baskin

I hope that you are able to find more value in your life through the information resonating inside this book. I do my best to provide content that is accurate, uplifting, and valuable to the reader. If you have any <u>constructive feedback</u> that you would like to offer, or feel like the content in my book can be <u>improved</u> in any way, please feel free to contact me at:

<u>faithinknowledge@bookenthuziast.com</u>

How to Overcome Rejection

★☆★FREE BONUS SECTION★☆★
'The Ultimate NLP Guide'

Rewards of NLP

Success is one of the most immediate rewards of NLP. There is virtually no limit to the reach of NLP in your life; it can be personal, professional, social, financial, spiritual, health and general well-being. Through NLP you can achieve personal success in the form of confidence and unlearning bad habits. Professional success can also be gained through job promotions and effective selling. Social success, such as with relationships and sensitivity, is also made possible. Financial success can be achieved when you are more in control of your decisions on earning, spending and saving. You can have a better or a more positive outlook in life enriching your spirituality. Health choices become improved and sustained.

Another set of rewards to those who practice NLP are those found in the path towards success. You develop better management skills, feel more motivated and enthusiastic and you can make sound and well-thought of decisions. You can identify, address, accept or surpass your limitation. You can make yourself more receptive by opening your minds towards new learning and beliefs. You develop coping skills to everyday stresses in life.

Perhaps, the most important reward of NLP is that you are able to change from within. Sometimes, people overestimate the effect of the outside world to them. They think that they are forever bound by the will of those around them. In fact, instead of the world affecting you, the truth is that you affect the world. The promotion you may have missed is not because of the decision of top management but because you projected a lack of confidence or failed in asserting yourself among your colleagues. This passivity is what caused the top management to choose another person over you.

When you retake control of yourself and change yourself from within, you can exude the change in your immediate environment. From there, the world will change in your favor. Of course, changing yourself from within is easier said than done. The changes cannot be done overnight and it must not be done haphazardly. Unguided, the change you make may prove disadvantageous to you down the road. NLP provides the map through which you can change yourself towards your true development and improvement.

For more information, go to: <u>http://amzn.to/1JJJeO8</u>

John Baskin

About the Author

Hi fellow reader,

My name is John Baskin and I am a student of life and love, seeing the world as one great experiment. I've lived a large portion of my life making decisions based on the opinions of others, which led to discontent and bitterness because I wasn't living in line with what truly resonates with me and, though people around me may not have been able to see that, the truth was revealed during moments of solitude.

I picked up journaling during my latter years in college and it became a ritual for me to record anything that came to mind. Though I was never an exceptional student of English during my academic years, I see writing as a way to express myself and it's been very therapeutic for me. I love the concept of journaling because it allows me to put all of my thoughts down and then look at them from an outsider's perspective, which allows me to identify patterns of thinking that are either empowering or disempowering the way I live. It is journaling that fuels my writing and I believe that a life worth living is worth recording.

As a fan of psychology and the personal development arena, I have a passion for creating deep connections, understanding people's mentalities as best I can, and fostering the environment for them to discover the personal power they possess to transform their life and live with a surge of enthusiasm and fulfillment. My hope is that this energy will be conveyed in my writing.

For you to pick up one of my books, I take it to mean that you are interested in improving your standard of living, and I have great respect for someone who is committed to personal growth and strengthening that desire in others.

Cheers to your path to ever-expanding greatness,

John Baskin

PS: I do my best to provide content that is *accurate*, *uplifting*, and *valuable* to the reader. If you have any <u>constructive feedback</u> that you would like to offer, or feel like the content in my book can be <u>improved</u> in any way, please feel free to contact me at:

<u>faithinknowledge@bookenthuziast.com</u>

How to Overcome Rejection

27797441R00074

Printed in Great Britain
by Amazon